# WORDS

OF

# POWER

*Also by John Woolley*
*and published by Arthur James*

I Am With You

Sorrow Into Joy

Prayers for the Family

The Friendship of Jesus

God's Secret

# WORDS
## OF
# POWER

John Woolley

ARTHUR JAMES
JOHN HUNT PUBLISHING
NEW ALRESFORD
1999

First published in Great Britain in 1999 by

ARTHUR JAMES
an imprint of
JOHN HUNT PUBLISHING
46a West Street, New Alresford, Hants SO24 9AU
United Kingdom

The author would like to thank John Lynch and Philip Law
for help in the preparation of this book.

John A. Woolley asserts the moral right
to be identified as the author of this work.

A catalogue record for this book is available
from the British Library.

ISBN 0 85305 450 9

Typeset in Adobe Goudy by
Strathmore Publishing Services, London N7

Printed and bound by
Tien Wah Press, Singapore

# Contents

# Preface

It is fascinating to look through the Bible for 'direct quotes' from God. We find lots of these in the Old Testament, of course, and then, through the mouth of Jesus our Lord, in the New Testament.

This little book brings together many of the verses in which God speaks directly to our need, helping us to chart a safe path as His followers.

After we have meditated on each set of verses there is a suggested prayer to help us to respond to what He is telling us on a specific theme. I have found, like so many others, that there is tremendous *power* in any verse in which God speaks directly.

We may take one subject each day – unhurriedly – but we can, of course, use the book in any way we wish. God's word is very versatile!

I know that our Lord Himself will be received in a special way as we receive these words.

JOHN A. WOOLLEY
*London*, January 1999

# WORDS
# OF POWER

# Love's Power

I have loved you with an everlasting love.

Even the hairs on your head are all counted.

You are of more value than many sparrows.

As the Father has loved Me, so have
I loved you.

God loved the world so much …

Simply go on living in My love!

Jeremiah 31.3; Luke 12.7; Luke 12.7; John 15.9;
John 3.16; John 15.9.

*Lord, I thank You that there is no love to compare with Yours!*

*Thank You that every detail of my life is known to You, every detail is Your concern.*

*Lord, help me to reflect, often, upon Your love's unchanging nature.*

*Let me remember, each day, Your love's constant and active influence, in and around me – shielding, strengthening, healing, peace-giving, enlightening, destructive of evil …*

*Let me always see Your love as being at the heart of all creation …*

# Seen Perfectly

I will come and live among you!

Before Abraham was, I AM!

Whoever has seen Me, has seen the Father.

I and the Father are One.

All things are given into My hand by the Father.

All power is Mine in heaven and on earth.

I am the Light of the world.

I am the bright morning Star.

Zechariah 2.10; John 8.58; John 14.9; John 10.30;
Matthew 11.27; Matthew 28.18; John 8.12;
Revelation 22.16.

God, our Father, when You revealed
Yourself, perfectly, in our world in Jesus
our Lord, it was history's decisive moment.

That moment in history begins for us true
knowledge of the great mystery of creation;
that moment gives me hope – the only real
hope that there is in this life.

Let me never cease to wonder at the love,
the purity, the greatness, which I see in the
Saviour of the world; let me keep Your
coming to earth close to my heart.

May I never – even for the briefest time
– stop trusting the Lord Jesus Christ as
the very centre of my life.

# Divine Initiative

You are drawn by me, with bands of love.

I have brought you to Myself with loving-kindness.

I have called you by your name. You belong to Me.

Because I chose you, I will wear you as one would a signet ring.

I know My sheep!

I will be a Father to you – you will be My children.

Hosea 11.4; Jeremiah 31.3; Isaiah 43.1; Haggai 2.23; John 10.14; 2 Corinthians 6.18.

Dear Lord, I would not have fixed my hope upon You if You had not first chosen me as one whom You would draw to Yourself.

Help me to value that choosing.

Help me to realize that Your choice means the privilege of experiencing Your love, and of finding a sense of purpose.

As I trust You, I realize that Your choice means my attaining perfection one day, Your drawing me into eventual oneness with Yourself.

Dear Lord, thank You for our indivisibility; may there be more of Your involvement – less and less of the old failing self ...

# Seeking Us

Return to Me ... I have bought your freedom.

Look to Me ... and be saved.

There is no other Saviour.

I came to search for the lost, and to save them.

I stand at the door and knock ...

I, the Lord, will save; I will rejoice over you.

I have found my sheep which was lost.

Isaiah 44.22; Isaiah 45.22; Isaiah 45.21; Luke 19.10;
Revelation 3.20; Zephaniah 3.17; Luke 15.6.

*Dear Lord, thank You that Your search is relentless.*

*Thank You that You sought me …*

*May I always be grateful that You found me!*

*Please accept my imperfect response to the love which wishes me to leave the past buried, and to live as a new person.*

*Help me, always, to be thrilled whenever I think of You …*

*Thank You that Your love never grows tired, as does human love.*

*Help me to build my life, increasingly, upon that which is unchanging.*

# Standing Invitation

You who are thirsty, come and drink!

I am the door …

If you knock, the door will be opened.

Come to Me …

How I have longed to gather you … as a hen gathers her chickens under her wings.

You must be born again!

No one comes to the Father except through Me.

Isaiah 55.1; John 10.29; Matthew 7.7;
Matthew 11.28; Matthew 23.37; John 3.3; John 14.6.

Lord, I believe that the door always stands
open for me to return, after going astray.
But help me to realize when I am stepping
into danger, and to return quickly.

I believe that Your invitation is not only
for those who do not know You, but a
permanent call to all Your children to
find renewal and refreshment, every day.

Help me to respond to Your invitation by
keeping my eyes upon You, looking always
into the light of Your presence.

May my joy be found, above all, in Your
welcoming presence and in Your utter
dependability.

# Love Indestructible

There is no greater love than when a person lays down his life for his friends.

For the sake of My sheep I am surrendering My life.

If I am lifted up from the earth, I will draw all to Myself.

John 15.13; John 10.15; John 12.32.

*Lord Jesus, thank You that You did
not merely speak of God's love; You
demonstrated it.*

*May my spirit be uplifted every day as
I imaginatively stand at the foot of Your
Cross, and hear You speak my name.*

*Help me to see all my pride, my impurity,
my coldness, my fickleness, borne by
Yourself, as Lamb of God.*

*Lord, Your love could not be crushed by
the power of darkness.*

*I know that, in return for Your love, You
ask, above all, that I simply offer You the
gift of my heart.*

*Thank You that every imperfect attempt to
follow Your way, every moment when I turn
to You in my need, can still comfort Your
heart.*

# Love's Obligation

I am the Lord your God, so infinitely patient, so forgiving ...

My thoughts towards you are those of peace.

Your sins may be like scarlet, but they shall be white as snow.

I revive the spirits of those who are humble, and renew the courage of those who show true sorrow.

I have blotted out your sins; I will not remember them!

His father ran out and embraced him!

Exodus 34.6; Jeremiah 29.11; Isaiah 1.18;
Isaiah 57.15; Isaiah 43.25; Luke 15.20.

$L$ord, whenever I feel that absence of peace which comes from wrong ways not laid before You, help me never to wait one moment before seeking Your forgiveness.

Help me never to doubt that when sorrow over wrong ways is deep, forgiveness simply pours out of You!

Thank You, Lord, for the miracle of Your love being strongly felt, even when that love has been hurt.

Only You can make times of repentance into times of encouragement and renewal!

# Love's Requirement

Be merciful ... as your heavenly Father is merciful.

... until seventy times seven!

If you forgive others, you will be forgiven.

Pray for those who ill-treat you.

Be reconciled with your brother ...

When you stand praying, first forgive.

Be at peace with one another.

Be good to those who hate you.

Luke 6.36; Matthew 18.22; Matthew 6.14;
Matthew 5.44; Matthew 5.24; Mark 11.25;
Mark 9.50; Matthew 5.44.

*L*ord, however hurt I feel, no matter how strong is the sense of being wronged, I cannot run away from Your demand upon me.

… the imperative that I should always be forgiving.

When I find it hard to forgive, let me borrow Your love in order to do it. Let me surrender all resentment, surrounding anyone, living or dead.

Let me, wherever possible, try my utmost to be reconciled – whatever the response of another person might be.

Lord, as I pray for anyone about whom I feel resentment, may I appreciate the supernatural evil power which attempts to drive people into unloving, hostile ways.

May I show, towards others, the same patience and understanding which I always receive from You.

# Love's Healing

I will heal all that they have done and love them freely.

The Son of Righteousness will rise upon you with healing in His wings.

It is I, Myself; do not be afraid.

I am the Lord who heals and restores you.

I will save the helpless ones.

They will not need to be afraid again!

I will give you rest for your soul.

That in Me you might have peace.

Hosea 14.4; Malachi 4.2; Matthew 14.27;
Exodus 15.26; Zephaniah 3.19; Jeremiah 23.4.
Matthew 11.28; John 16.33.

Dear Lord, I believe that any healing outside Your love is only partial.

As I live in Your love, I know that there is a restoring influence upon spirit, mind and body.

Thank You, Lord, for the healing peace which comes with Your forgiveness.

Thank You for the love I experience as You share earth's dark places with me.

Thank You for everything which has helped me to appreciate that love ...

# Mind Made Up

Whoever believes in Me will live!

Do you believe in the Son of God?

Happy are those who have not seen Me, but believe.

Do not be without faith … believe!

I pray for all those who will become believers.

Whoever believes in Me will never again be thirsty.

I have prayed for you, that your faith will not desert you.

When the Son of Man comes, will He find faith on the earth?

John 11.25; John 9.35; John 20.29; John 20.27;
John 17.20; John 6.35; Luke 22.32; Luke 18.8.

*Lord Jesus, may I always be like those of whom You spoke to Thomas ... not having seen You, but believing. You know just how strong my belief can be and, at times, just how wavering!*

*May that belief never disappear completely.*

*I realize that believing means life, though the way is often hard.*

*I sense that unbelief is really a living death. Give me the will to believe, whatever my fluctuating feelings.*

*Help me to discern Your working in a dark world, making everything serve a good purpose for those who place their confidence in You.*

# Faithful

I will hear your prayers.

I will never forget you; your image is on the palms of My hands.

A mother may forget her child, but I will not forget you!

I will not fail you.

I will remember my promises to you.

Your strength will be found in quietness and confidence.

I will care for you to the end.

Jeremiah 29.12; Isaiah 49.16; Isaiah 49.15;
Joshua 1.5; Genesis 9.16; Isaiah 30.15; Isaiah 46.4.

Dear Lord, how can I fail to trust Someone who always has me in His thoughts?

I believe that Your love makes it impossible for You to fail me.

I believe that You are constantly bringing about what You see is right for my life.

I will go on believing this, even when I find it hard to grasp what You are doing, or to understand what You are allowing.

I believe, too, that You are bringing about what You see is best for those about whom I am concerned, those for whom I pray. May I never delay that process!

Lord, I thank You for present circumstances as within Your answers to my prayers.

I intuitively thank You that I will never prove trust in You to be misplaced.

# All-embracing

I am the Lord – the first and the last.

Is not My presence everywhere?

With whom will you compare Me?

I do not change.

With God, all things are possible.

Is anything too hard for Me?

Without Me, you can do nothing.

God in the midst of you is a mighty Saviour.

Isaiah 41.4; Jeremiah 23.24; Isaiah 40.25; Malachi 3.6; Mark 10.27; Genesis 18.14; John 15.5; Zephaniah 3.17.

Dear Lord, it is so easy to speak of Your greatness, but so hard to act upon it!

When courage seems to be deserting me, when I seem unable to change direction from ways of a lifetime, let me unite myself, very deliberately with Your greatness. Help me to see our unity!

Let the thought that the Creator of this universe (and beyond) is on my side through this life, give me new confidence.

Lord, help me to bring to You, immediately, every burden, every complexity, every challenging circumstance – knowing that You will both share, and give me victory.

Thinking much of Your greatness, may I learn simply to rise above circumstances.

# Every Need

I am your great reward.

I came that you might have life ...
abundantly!

Light has come into the world ...

The water which I give to you is like a
well, springing up into eternal life.

If the Son sets you free, you really are free.

Genesis 15.1; John 10.10; John 3.19;
John 4.13; John 8.36.

*Lord, how can I thank You for all that
I possess if I have You?*


*I have all the resources of God!
    You shine on me in a world of
        complexity;
    You set me free from evil's power;
    You open for me a whole new existence
        of freedom;
    You give life whenever I turn to You;
    You are there in the foreground of life
        when I merely whisper Your Name.
    You are my unequalled source of
        understanding;
    You are the one gift which is beyond
        price!*

# First Claim

Let your true satisfaction lie in
knowing Me.

Do not seek great things for yourself.

Your heart will be where your treasure is …

… make sure your treasure is in heaven.

I must be first in your affections.

Finding one precious pearl, he sold everything so that he could buy it.

No one can serve two masters …

What gain is there in gaining the whole
world and losing your soul?

Jeremiah 9.24; Jeremiah 45.5; Matthew 6.21;
Matthew 6.20; Exodus 20.3; Matthew 13.46;
Matthew 6.24; Mark 8.36.

28

*Lord, the world contains so much that dazzles. Even when I learn to see through some of life's deceptions, I am still tempted to pursue false goals.*

*Please break any attachment to desires and objectives which do not serve Your purposes.*

*Help me always to put You first, and then to see everything else in relation to this.*

*Help me to remember that even when I lose all sources of support, but still have You, I have everything.*

*Help me, when earth's support fails, to feed upon Your unchanging love.*

# Childlike

Whoever does not receive the Kingdom of God as a little child, will not enter.

If you believe, anything is possible.

Whatever you ask in prayer, believe that you have it and it will be so.

Ask ... and it will be given to you.

If you live in Me and My word lives in you, ask whatever you wish and it will be done for you.

According to your faith, may it happen for you!

Mark 10.15; Mark 9.23; Mark 11.24; Matthew 7.7; John 15.7; Matthew 9,29.

*Lord, the paradox is that 'childlike' means true maturity!*

*You gave us no option but to cultivate simplicity and expectancy and to surrender pride, and worldly sophistication.*

*May I always believe the very best of You, and leave every area of life open for Your working.*

*May I never forget the duty to thank You for everything which You allow, as I go on trusting You.*

*Lord, show me that for which I am right to ask, that which You want for me.*

# Unfailing

I will satisfy My people with My goodness.

The birds, who do not sow, are fed by your heavenly Father.

Your Father knows what you need!

Your heavenly Father will give good things to those who ask Him.

Before My children call, I will answer.

I, Myself, am the wealth which you need.

I am the Bread of Life.

They will call upon My name and I will hear them.

Jeremiah 31.14; Matthew 6.26; Matthew 6.8;
Matthew 7.11; Isaiah 65.24; Numbers 18.20;
John 6.35; Zechariah 13.9.

*Lord Jesus, help me not to waver in*
*believing Your promise that if I put Your*
*cause first, all that I ever really need will*
*come to me.*

*Help me to recognize Your provision in*
*the happenings of each day ...*
> *each meeting,*
> *each danger averted,*
> *each unexpected supply,*
> *each experience of peace which*
> > *contradicts the circumstances*
> > *of the moment.*

*Thank You that all the time You are*
*answering my prayers in the best*
*possible way.*

*Thank You that You are the origin of every*
*good thing in my life.*

# Made Strong

I will accompany you, and prosper everything which you undertake.

I will hold you by your right hand.

It will not be by mere strength, but by My Spirit.

It is in your weakness that My strength is made perfect.

To bear fruit, the branch must remain united with the vine.

I am the vine; you are the branches.

Exodus 33.14; Isaiah 41.13; Zechariah 4.6;
2 Corinthians 12.9; John 15.4; John 15.5.

*Lord, let me never lose a sense of
dependency upon You.*

*Help my realization of where I am weak
open the way for Your power to flow.*

*Let my using of Your strength become
instinctive.*

*May I allow You to complete every victory
for me.*

*May I find gains in areas which once
defeated me completely – and then hold
on to those gains.*

*Lord, let me keep that sense of being united
with You.*

*I know that You go ahead of me to remove
obstacles not yet imagined.*

*Lord, please go with me into every challenge.*

# Victory Assured

I am the Lord your God – your Saviour!

The Prince of this world will be overthrown.

I saw Satan fall as lightning from heaven.

... *kept* from evil.

Whoever endures to the end will be saved.

You will be opposed but not overcome,
because I am with you to save you.

I give you power over the Enemy's power!

Be alert and pray ...

Isaiah 43.3; John 12.31; Luke 10.18; John 17.15;
Matthew 24.13; Jeremiah 1.19; Luke 10.19;
Matthew 26.41.

*L*ord Jesus, let me never underestimate
the activity of evil in this world.

Help me to remember that, in spite of evil's
apparent successes, its days are numbered.

Because of Your victory I truly am already
saved from the worst that evil can do, as
I make that victory mine. Where You are
trusted, evil is powerless.

Each day, may I consciously convert evil's
attacks into wonderful victories.

Help me to recognize – immediately – all
that is not of You, all that represents subtle
temptation.

When tempted, may I remember to look
away to You, lifted above the temptation.

Thank You, Lord, for all the unnoticed
dangers through which You bring me
each day.

# Supported

I am with you to save you.

I will let no one oppose you.

I will be with you in times of trouble to rescue you.

I made you, and will be able to carry you!

In this present world you will experience trouble and sorrow. But rejoice! I have conquered the world.

Do not let your heart be troubled or afraid.

I am with you always.

Jeremiah 1.19; Joshua 1.5; Psalm 91.15; Isaiah 46.4; John 16.33; John 14.27; Matthew 28.20.

When life is overwhelming, help me, Lord,
to turn – automatically – to You.

Let me allow You to lead me through the
chaos towards the light – even though light
may be temporarily hidden.

Even in the darkest places, teach me not
to be afraid.

Let the thought of Your presence in my
future be projected into every present
need-situation.

May I never let anxiety build up by looking
at life merely from my limited human stand-
point.

Lord, may I firmly hold to the promise that
I have nothing to fear.

# Secure

I am the Good Shepherd.

No one can take My children out of My hand.

Do not be afraid because I accompany you.

I will be with you when you go through deep waters.

I am with you, wherever you go.

My sheep shall go in and out and find pasture.

When you pass through fire, it will not burn you.

John 10.14; John 10.28; Isaiah 41.10; Isaiah 43.2;
Joshua 1.9; John 10.9; Isaiah 43.2.

Lord, I realize that earthly security can fail
– often unexpectedly.

I believe Your word that I cannot be
separated from You – that You surround
me, when I experience life's more frightening
aspects.

Lord, help me to see every present difficulty
against the background of Your eternity.

Let my fear melt in the thought of Your love.

Let me see Your love as a fortress – when
I have nowhere to fly to but to Yourself.

# Illuminated

Your sadness will be turned into joy.

Tell the prisoners that they can come out!

Your sun will never set.

Little flock, you must not be afraid.

I will not leave you comfortless.

Blessed are those in great sadness ...
they will be comforted.

I am making everything new!

John 16.20; Isaiah 49.9; Isaiah 60.20; Luke 12.32;
John 14.18; Matthew 5.4; Revelation 21.5.

*Lord Jesus, everything about You*
*represents change from darkness to light.*

*I know that where You are trusted, earth's*
*sorrows will one day turn into an unending*
*bliss.*

*Thank You for helping us to find hope again*
*when life leaves us shattered and full of*
*doubt.*

*Help me to see that the transition from*
*the despair of the Cross to the joy of Your*
*Resurrection can be a pattern for me on*
*many occasions during this present life.*

# Green Pastures

I am the shepherd of My sheep and cause them to rest.

Do not be concerned about tomorrow.

Will all your worries add one moment to your life!?

You will be led beside water-springs.

Consider the lilies of the field!

I am meek and humble of heart.

My people will live in peace … in quiet resting-places.

Come to some quiet place, and rest for a while.

Ezekiel 34.15; Matthew 6.34;
Matthew 6.27; Isaiah 49.10; Matthew 6.28;
Matthew 11.29; Isaiah 32.18; Mark 6.31.

*Lord, help me to stop striving!*

*Help me to rest my spirit in You, because You never stop working for me.*

*Make me content to be led by the good Shepherd, who knows precisely what will make for my true fulfilment and contentment.*

*Let my life be a copy of Yours, increasingly.*

*Let the pace of my life more closely resemble Your own.*

*I will remember to make a fresh giving of my present and future to You every day.*

# Sole Standard

There is no other God.

All who love the truth are My followers.

To know the truth will set you free!

… leading you into all truth …

The Spirit of truth … will be in you.

I am the Way.

I am Truth.

Isaiah 45.6; John 18.37; John 8.32; John 16.13;
John 14.17; John 14.6; John 14.6.

*Lord, grant me to see as You see ... may
I have the eye of truth.*

*May I clearly see that which You in-dwell
and recognize that which is corrupted by evil.*

*Make me aware of times when choices which
You see as vital are being made.*

*Lord, help me never to compromise with
truth.*

*May I never live at variance with what I
know in my heart to be true.*

*May I always remain faithful to the truth
which You have revealed.*

*At all times, and above everything else, may
I hold firmly to the truth of Your unchanging
love.*

# Wisdom Gained

My sheep recognize My voice.

I put before you the way of life and the way of death.

I, the Lord God, will be your everlasting light.

If you follow Me, you will never walk in the dark.

I will both guide and instruct you.

Do not be complacent in your wisdom.

My thoughts are not your thoughts.

Walk in the light! …

John 10.27; Jeremiah 21.8; Isaiah 60.19; John 8.12;
Psalm 32.8; Jeremiah 9.23; Isaiah 55.8; John 12.35.

*Lord, sometimes bewilderment is intense, as I try to follow Your way.*

*I know that evil tries to confuse in many subtle ways.*

*Often the choices of life are painful; often they lie between pleasing You and pleasing someone near to me.*

*May I always be utterly resigned to your will and learn to let You enlighten every finely-balanced choice.*

*May I carefully look at everything by the light of Your presence.*

*Let me always surrender to Your control of events, and never fear the results of action after waiting upon You.*

*When an awareness of the way forward is still withheld from me for a good reason of Your own, give me that trust that You are leading and will intervene to bring about Your wishes.*

# Divine Guest

My Spirit will never leave you.

I will give you a new heart and a new spirit.

We will make our home in him!

Happy are those with pure hearts;
they shall see God.

I in you ...

Pruning you to make you even more fruitful.

It is the Spirit which gives life.

... that you may be children of light!

A corrupt tree cannot produce good fruit.

The Kingdom of God is within you.

Isaiah 59.21; Ezekiel 36.26; John 14.23; Matthew 5.8;
John 15.4; John 15.2; John 6.63; John 12.36;
Matthew 7.18; Luke 17.21.

$I$t is wonderful to know, Lord, that You not only surround me, but that You live in me by Your Spirit.

I open myself to the work of Your Spirit – allowing You to make everything new, making me ready for the life with You which You have promised.

In spite of times of failure, let me never doubt progress as You work in me.

May Your presence in me show up all that needs to be driven from my life; let me grieve over such things and form a strong resolve that they must go.

Lord, let Your presence – and my willing-ness – ensure that all impediments to a closer walk with You are removed.

# Path of Safety

Happy are those who are hungry and thirsty for goodness.

If your right eye causes you to go astray, pluck it out.

You must be perfect!

Be holy – for I am holy.

The way leading to life is narrow.

Wear My yoke – it is easy.

If you keep My commands, you will live in My love.

Hearing the word of God and keeping it means true happiness.

If you act on My words, you are like the wise man who built on rock.

Go in by the narrow gate!

Matthew 5.6; Matthew 18.9; Matthew 5.48;
1 Peter 1.16; Matthew 7.14; Matthew 11.30;
John 15.10; Luke 11.28; Matthew 7.24;
Matthew 7.14.

Lord Jesus, the further I go with You, the more I realize how narrow must be the way – so great are the dangers.

Thank You for Your Victory which secured for me the power to choose.

I believe that wearing Your yoke can never be as hard as trying to meet life without You.

May I have a joyful acceptance of Your will.

I believe that Your strength is automatically there whenever I decide upon Your way.

I believe that every effort in obedience which I make is completed by You.

Lord, make me very teachable, ready to act upon lessons learned.

*Whenever I have acted without You,*
*whenever I have wanted only my own*
*way, please over-rule, for Your love's sake.*

# Grateful

Go to your friends and tell them what the Lord has done for you.

Whoever speaks well of Me to those around will find that I will speak well of that person before My Father in heaven.

You have kept My word and not denied My Name.

I will honour those who honour Me.

Mark 5.19; Matthew 10.32; Revelation 3.8;
1 Samuel 2.30.

May I never fail You, Lord, by neglecting to tell others, sensitively and enthusiastically, what You have done for me.

Let my sense of gratitude to You draw some longing heart towards finding You as life's answer.

Help me to remember my thanks to You each day, for what You do through me, even when I am conscious only of weakness.

Dear Lord, I offer all that I am, all that I have, for You and for Your children.

# Shining

You must let your light shine for those around you.

My Father is glorified by your bearing much fruit.

There is a large harvest, but few to send.

You are My servant and will bring glory to My name.

You are the world's salt!

… that men may see your good works and give glory to your Father in heaven.

Matthew 5.16; John 15.8; Matthew 9.37;
Isaiah 49.3; Matthew 5.13; Matthew 5.16.

*Lord, there is so much need ...*

*May I always put myself at Your disposal.*

*Let me live so close to You that I can take for granted that You are working through me, and extending the influence of Your love.*

*Lord, give me the will to be loving – to reflect Your love – even when there are clouds over my life.*

*May everything be for Your glory alone.*

*Help me – with greater than human understanding – to discern need in others; may they, above all, come to experience Your love.*

# God Conveyed

Hearing the word, receiving it, and producing much fruit.

Heaven and earth will disappear, but My word will endure.

My word accomplishes My purposes.

… those who hear God's word and keep it!

The words I speak to you are Spirit-filled and mean life.

Knowing these things, you will be happy if you act on them.

Happy are those whom the Lord will find waiting for Him!

Mark 4.20; Matthew 24.35; Isaiah 55.11; Luke 11.28;
John 6.63; John 13.17; Luke 12.37.

*Dear Lord, I can only prove the power of Your word by basing my actions upon it – blindly.*

*Relying upon Your word, may I always act trustingly not merely feeling trust.*

*Let me be fed by Your word, strengthened by it, increasingly.*

*May Your word not only point the way, but bring more and more of Yourself into the deepest parts of me.*

*May Your word unfailingly bring healing to my spirit.*

*Lord, I stake everything upon Your word – just as I stake everything upon You.*

*I am certain, from Your word, that I belong to You for ever!*

# Indispensable

Only one thing is vital …

My Kingdom is not of this world.

When you earnestly seek Me,
you will find Me.

Seek Me and live.

… I will meet with you!

Wait upon Me, listen to Me,
and your soul shall live.

I live in the holy places, with those of
a humble spirit.

Luke 10.42; John 18.36; Jeremiah 29.13; Amos 5.4;
Exodus 25.22; Isaiah 55.3; Isaiah 57.15.

*Lord, I know that making time for You*
*– just where I am – must be a vital part*
*of each day.*

*As I turn to You, at any time, I know that*
*You have turned, already, to meet me!*

*In those times of communion with you,*
*I take into myself all that You are …*
  *I find Your light shining upon my*
    *circumstances, helping me to see*
    *things in proportion;*
  *I can bring others' needs before You;*
  *I become sure that my prayers can create*
    *new situations;*
  *I can find Your peace to penetrate present*
    *circumstances;*
  *I can be sure of there being more and*
    *more of what is of You in me.*

*Lord, help me to remember how each turning*
*to You meets Your longing!*

# His Reward

Whoever overcomes will inherit all things.

Well done, good and faithful servant!

Kept for you in heaven is a treasure which will not fail you.

I will satisfy My people with My goodness.

It is My Father's good pleasure to give you the Kingdom.

Fix your mind on God's Kingdom and His justice above everything.

Come, you who are blessed of My Father!

In My Father's Kingdom, good people will shine like the sun.

Revelation 21.7; Matthew 25.21; Luke 12.33;
Jeremiah 31.14; Luke 12.32; Matthew 6.33;
Matthew 25.34; Matthew 13.43.

*Lord Jesus, thank You that I cannot see, precisely, what lies ahead.*

*Whatever happens, help me to go on serving You – even when thoroughly disheartened – bringing the divine love to others.*

*Help me to keep in mind that You reward persistence.*

*Lord, help me to endure; help me to hear already, within my heart, Your words of welcome when I complete my journey.*

# Realization

I am creating new heavens, and a new earth.

In My Father's house are many dwelling-places.

I am going now to prepare a place for you.

I will receive you ...

To be with Me where I am, and to see My glory!

I will give the fountain of the water of life, freely.

... so that your joy may be complete.

No one will be able to take your joy from you.

Isaiah 65.17; John 14.2; John 14.2; John 14.3; John 17.24; Revelation 21.6; John 16.24; John 16.22.

*L*ord, thank You for all that You are
preparing for me.


When I am where You dwell, I know that
I shall desire nothing else!


My treasure will be Yourself …


I know that the joy which I can experience
by remaining true to You will last for ever.


Lord, help many to find that joy.

*Other books from John Woolley*

# I AM WITH YOU

Since 1984 people throughout the world have been discovering the power to change lives of the little devotional book, *I Am With You*.

The divinely inspired words bring a sense of our Lord's presence, in a wonderful way, to strengthen the reader in his or her personal need.

*I commend this little book to all who are seeking to deepen their spiritual lives.*
– Cardinal Basil Hume, England

I Am With You *is a very special book; it will bless countless people.*
– Prebendary John Pearce, England

*I have never experienced such a closeness to Jesus.*
– Fran Gunning, USA

*A lovely book of devotions; we use it daily.*
– Dr Donald English,
former President, Methodist Conference

I Am With You *will deeply touch many people.*
– Fr. Robert de Grandis, USA

*The most wonderful book I have ever read.*
– Fr. Tom Cass, England

## SORROW INTO JOY

Since the publication of the well-loved devotional classic, *I Am With You*, further words from the risen Lord Jesus Christ have been received by Fr. John in times of prayer.

*Sorrow Into Joy* takes us into the mystery of the suffering which so many endure today. We look anew at the power of the Cross, and at the love which still shines in the world's darkness.

Our Lord's words give us courage, as we glimpse the eternity when all things will be made new.

## GOD'S SECRET

The way in which we see God's relationship with us can be revolutionized by reading this book.

So many struggling Christians have not come across 'God's secret' and the way in which His love can *affect* us.

This book will open a new dimension in our thinking – combined with practical ways of immediately making what we are learning part of our lives. The result? A larger place for the love of Jesus in our hearts, whoever we are!

# THE FRIENDSHIP OF JESUS

Already this book has helped many (of all ages)
to find life's one vital friendship.

The book was written, firstly, for those with
little or no faith, and secondly for 'believers'
wanting to experience Jesus more warmly. As
we follow the very simple steps, God will be at
work to bring about a *lasting* friendship.

The Friendship of Jesus *is extremely helpful.*
*I doubt if anyone could fail to profit*
*from reading it.*
– Dr Stuart Blanch,
former Archbishop of York

*This lovely book.*
– Canadian reader

*This book is both very beautiful and very*
*practical – a rare combination. It gives us new*
*insights whenever it is read or re-read.*
*What a friend we have in Jesus!*
– London reader

*I have seen lives wonderfully changed*
*by this little book.*
– Church leader, South of England

*I just couldn't put the book down.*
– Asian immigrant,
becoming a Christian

# PRAYERS FOR THE FAMILY

There is a very familiar saying that 'families which pray together, stay together.'

If, from the earliest days, older and younger can share prayer-times, they become aware of God's provision and protection for that family in a very special way; they become sure that He is interested in every detail of that family's existence.

Using these prayers, boys and girls can progress from saying them with their parents, or older relatives, into making up their own prayers. It is not long before the young ones enjoy the daily habit of talking with Jesus on their own.